Frederik Meissner

Sustainable business models
in the context of the
circular economy

How can a company produce and deliver products using sustainable methods?

Bibliografische Information der Deutschen Nationalbibliothek:

Die Deutsche Nationalbibliothek verzeichnet diese Publikation in der Deutschen Nationalbibliografie; detaillierte bibliografische Daten sind im Internet über http://dnb.d-nb.de abrufbar.

Impressum:

Copyright © Science Factory 2020

Ein Imprint der GRIN Publishing GmbH, München

Druck und Bindung: Books on Demand GmbH, Norderstedt, Germany

Covergestaltung: GRIN Publishing GmbH

Abstract

This bachelor thesis contains a case study of two Business Models in the mobile phone industry. This industry is an example for the responsibility Business Models have concerning the excessive use of resources and negative social impacts by exploiting workers in manufacturing companies and in the mining industry. We select two Business Models whose aim is to produce and deliver products using "sustainable" methods. The first case is the smartphone retailer Fairphone, who provides a long-living, modular, and transparent mobile phone. The second case is Mazuma Mobile, a refurbishment service that provides second-hand mobile phones and the possibility to sell an old or broken electronic device. In the analysis, we conduct a case study based on Osterwalder's Business Model Canvas, containing Nine Building Blocks that explain the business logic a company. The goal is to better understand how companies propose, create, deliver, and capture value. We select the Circular Economy and their principles in order to assess the sustainability of the cases in the discussion. The Circular Economy is seen as a condition and a beneficial relation for sustainability. Discussing the question of how the Business Models correspond to the principles of the Circular Economy leads us to the conclusion that there are improvements necessary in both cases. Nevertheless, the modular design of Fairphone provides self-made repairing possibilities, long use, and recycling and reusing activities are implemented by partners. The transparent value chain leads to an improvement of the working conditions and exploitation of resources. The gap-exploiting model of Mazuma Model reveals a lack in the industry and extends the life of mobile phones. The company focuses on reusing, refurbishing, and recycling activities and since millions of unused mobile phones exist, the company is crucial for the development in a circular direction.

Table of Contents

Table of Figures

List of Tables

1 Introduction

"If it can't be reduced, reused, repaired,

Rebuilt, refurbished, refinished, resold,

Recycled or composted

Then it should be restricted, redesigned

Or removed from production."

– Song by Pete Seeger in 2008

This song by Pete Seeger has not been written particularly for the mobile phone industry, but still deploys a realistic vision of it. Can you imagine that people in Germany store around 124 million mobile phones at home without using them (Bitkom, 2018)? Retailers sell hardware for low prices, combined with long-term contracts. This industry is an example of how a business model leads to excessive use of resources with a negative social impact. The consequence is an excessive use of resources because a mobile phone includes raw materials such as rare earths and the so-called conflict minerals. Tin, tantalum (cobalt), tungsten, and gold are the most commonly mined conflict minerals also known as "3TG". The negative social impacts stem from bad working conditions in manufacturing companies in China and the conditions in the mining industry (Boons & Lüdeke-Freund, 2013). The challenges around sustainability, the use of conflict minerals, the repairability and the reduction of waste have become part of the public debate and smartphone manufacturer are pressured to develop more sustainable systems of production (OECD, 2012; Dießenbacher & Reller, 2016). However, this is not only a problem of the mobile phone industry, but the linear model of resource production and consumption is a global economic problem (EMF, 2012). In 2010, 65 billion tons of raw materials were processed by the economic system. In 2020, this amount is expected to increase to 82 billion tons, which would correspond to 8.2 million times the Eiffel Tower (EMF, 2012; Spiegel Online, 2017). It is obvious that we are in dire need of changing this linear system of using materials to manufacture products for consumers to dump the products when they no longer serve their purpose.

This bachelor thesis contains a case study which analyzes two Business Models (BM) in the mobile phone industry that have declared their goal to produce and distribute mobile phones using "sustainable" methods. Sustainability became an increasingly important concept for the strategies of companies and a goal of their development. It originates in the French verb "soutenir", which means to hold up or support (Brown et al., 1987). The first BM to analyze is the "Fairphone 2", a smartphone from the Netherlands. The company aims at producing a sustainable smartphone, focusing mostly on improvements in their supply chain management. The company is focused on long-lasting designs, materials that do not come from areas of conflict, reusing and recycling and safe working conditions in their supplying companies (Fairphone, 2018). Besides that, the Fairphone 2 is a modular designed phone. This means that a specific module of the hardware, e.g. the camera, can be changed if it is faulty, instead of changing the complete device. The second case is the company "Mazuma Mobile", an online service platform founded in 2006. The British company focuses on the collection, refurbishment, and sale of old or broken mobile phones. They buy old mobile phones from people, to directly resell or first refurbish them if necessary - in case the mobile phone cannot be reused, the company will recycle it (Mazuma Mobile, 2018). According to the company, they return the large majority of their received phones (~150,000 every month) back to the market (EMF, 2011).

In order to analyze the BMs of the described manufacturers, we conduct a case study in which we will apply Osterwalder's Business Model Canvas (2004) to the two cases. Business Model concepts have become a new unit to analyze the business logic of firms (Stähler, 2002) which can improve measuring, observing, and comparing the business of a firm. In Osterwalder's Canvas, the Business Models encompass Nine Building Blocks (BB) that can be comprised by three dimensions: the value proposition, the value creation and delivery, and the value capturing (Richardson, 2008; Osterwalder et al., 2005). In order to embed this analysis in the right context, we interpret the crucial findings of the analysis with the principles of the Circular Economy (CE). The conceptual relationship between sustainability and the CE is regarded as a beneficial relation, a trade-off, or even a condition for sustainability (Geissdoerfer et al., 2017). The CE can lead to sustainable development by minimizing resource inputs, waste, emission, and energy leakage (Mathews & Tan, 2011). The so-called "closing-the-loop" production, long-lasting design, maintenance, repair, reuse, remanufacturing, refurbishing or recycling are ways to achieve a circular system (Ghisellini et al., 2016; Geissdoerfer et al., 2017).

The paper is structured as follows. In the second chapter, we start with the theoretical foundation by giving an overview of the Circular Economy and Osterwalder's Business Model Canvas. This thesis is focused on mobile phones that are produced largely by using technical nutrients. Therefore, I highlighted the Technical

Cycle of the Circular Economy and the most common principles of the CE. This enables us to assess the BMs. In the third chapter, the two cases are shortly presented. For the analysis in the fourth chapter, Osterwalder's Business Model Canvas is crucial. The goal is to better understand how Fairphone and Mazuma Mobile propose, create, and deliver value based on the BM Canvas. The focus of the analysis is on the crucial BB, that enable circular developments. The Value Capturing (revenues and costs) is noted, but not deeply analyzed and discussed, due to the fact that they are not implemented in the BM in a circular way. Afterward, in the fifth chapter, we discuss and compare the circular developments of both cases and explain different outputs related to the principles and concepts of the CE that are based on the Technical Cycle of the Circular Economy, the three R's (Reduction, Reuse, Recycle) and the Design. Before we draw the conclusion, implications and limitations will be given as well.

2 Theoretical Foundation

2.1 The Circular Economy

In 1966, the CE was mentioned for the first time in academic literature by Boulding, an ecological economist. He proposed to use a circular material system as a way to guarantee human life on earth (Boulding, 1966). Pearce and Turner (1989) described on Boulding's idea how natural resources become the input for production and after they are consumed, the resources go to waste. At that time, it was already obvious that the traditional linear economy without recycling is not sustainable (Pearce & Turner, 1990). A few years before, Stahel and Reday (1976) formulated an industrial loop economy to show strategies for waste prevention, resource efficiency, regional job creation, and dematerialization in the economy. Stahel (1982) proposed to sell utilization instead of ownership, the first idea for a sustainable BMs in a loop economy, as well as the spiral-loop system in *Figure 1: The Self-Replenishing System*

(based on: Stahel 1984). This system shows a material production with virgin resources. Within the loops, resources should first be manufactured, then used, and finally replenished.

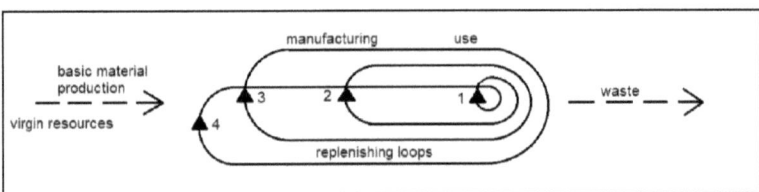

Figure 1: The Self-Replenishing System
(based on: Stahel 1984)

In recent years, the CE has increasingly drawn public attention to itself when it comes to discussing sustainability (Geissdoerfer et al., 2017; Lieder & Rashid, 2016). The potential of the CE can be a possibility to overcome the current linear production and consumption model that is known as the economy of "take, make, and dispose" (EMF, 2015). This means that companies take resources, e.g. raw materials, make a product out of it and the consumer disposes of it after using. One of the most popular definitions of the CE is:

"A circular economy is one that is restorative and regenerative by design and aims to keep products, components, and materials at their highest utility and value at all times, distinguishing between technical and biological cycles"

(EMF, 2012, p. 2).

This thesis will focus mainly on the technical cycle of the CE, which is explained in Figure 2: The Technical Cycle of the Circular Economy (adopted from: EMF 2012).

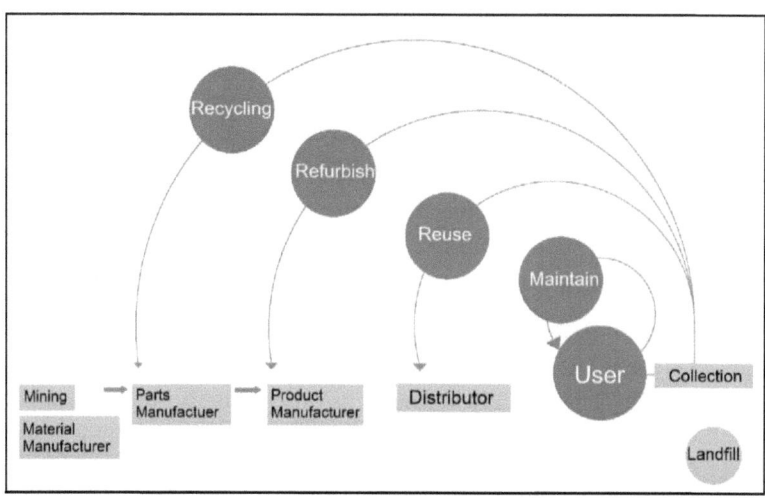

Figure 2: The Technical Cycle of the Circular Economy
(adopted from: EMF 2012

The Ellen MacArthur Foundation (EMF) designed the Technical Cycle of the Circular Economy comprising maintaining, reusing, refurbishing and recycling activities as an overview of how to use technical materials in the CE. The model works as follows. Mined or manufactured raw materials are delivered to the "parts manufacturer", who produces parts and delivers them to the "product manufacturer". The product manufacturer finishes the product and delivers it to the distributor (service provider). The distributor delivers the product to the customer/user. After using a product in the CE, the product is collected and allocated to the appropriate cycle. In other words, the product has to follow a principle contained in the CE. This is important for our analysis in the following. Sequentially, the main **principles of the Circular Economy** will be explained.

The **Maintaining** principle is applied when the use of a product is prolonged as long as possible and the product preserves most of its value. A product can follow the Maintaining principle as long as the product does not return back to the company. This principle comprises cleaning, repairing, and upgrading by the user (Van den Berg & Bakker, 2015). However, optimal maintenance starts with designing the product with lifetime prognostics in order to forecast the future performance of the product. Improvements in the original design of products can lead to scale economies and efficiency in the reverse cycle. Maintaining technical nutrients at higher quality throughout the cycles extends the longevity and overall material productivity (EMF, 2015).

The **Reduction** principle is part of the so-called three R's: Reduction, Reuse, and Recycle. Reduction means to improve the efficiency of production and consumption of waste, energy, and raw materials e.g. simplified packaging (Su et al., 2013). Next to the packaging, companies can increase their eco-efficiency (keep or increase the value of your product while reducing its environmental impact) on the production side. This strategy seeks to maximize the value of a good with decreased environmental impact (Figge et al., 2014).

The **Reusing** principle encompasses "any operation by which products or components that are not waste are used again for the same purpose for which they were conceived" (EU, 2008, p. 527). Product reuse also encompasses the product redistribution and implicates that the physical qualities and functions remain unchanged. Reusing leads to a product manufacturing that requires fewer resources, less energy, and less labor compared to products that are manufactured with virgin, or even recycled or disposal resources. This is attractive for companies in terms of environmental benefits (Castellani et al., 2015). Companies could implement incentives like take-back programs, fostering marketing of remanufactured products and the design of durable products for multiple cycles of use (Prendeville et al., 2014).

The **Refurbishing** principle comprises product repair, remanufacturing, and refurbishing. It describes the process of returning a product back to working. This can be achieved by replacing or repairing major components that are faulty. However, refurbishing is needed when the product is not directly reusable and first has to go back to the product manufacturer. Either the product can be used for the same purpose or it enters a remanufacturing system that takes back and dismantles it, so its parts and modules can be used as input for other products (EMF, 2015).

The **Recycling** principle is "any recovery operation by which waste materials are reprocessed into products, materials or substances whether for the original or other purposes. It includes the reprocessing of organic material but does not include energy recovery and the reprocessing into materials that are to be used as fuels or for backfilling operations" (EU, 2008, p. 527). Product recycling has to be considered when the product cannot be used again. The product has to be recycled and then delivered back to the appropriate manufacturer in the economy. Companies can extract resources through recycling and safe expensive mining of virgin resources. This recycling process of valuable resources is critically important in the mobile phone industry (Deutsche Umwelthilfe, 2018). Iron, aluminum, copper, gold, and platinum can be recycled in a profitable way, but other metals like gallium, indium, tantalum, or the rare-earth elements are less likely to be recycled. This is because of the complex and expensive recycling process and the fact that there are only small amounts used in the electronic devices (Deutsche Umwelthilfe, 2018). There is no official public information about how many devices are recycled by the companies in the mobile phone industry but metals like copper, iron, gold, and silver are often recycled because of the high value of these materials (Deutsche Umwelthilfe, 2018).

A general possibility to implement a circular system is the **Designing** principle. Products can be designed for maintenance, repairing, reusing, refurbishing, or recycling. The way the product is designed can already influence the number of raw materials and energy being used in its product lifecycle. Modularity provides a popular possibility to design a circular product or service. The basic idea has been part of older concepts like the "near-decomposability" concept. Near-decomposability means that a system should be divided into several parts organized in a hierarchical way (Simon, 1962). Modularity has different definitions and can be applied to several fields. In the case of smartphones, we understand it as product design modularity. This modularity provides a set of changeable hardware parts to allocate a maximum possibility of repair and minimum production of waste (Campagnolo & Camuffo, 2010). In general, tighter circles (e.g. maintain) are preferable to broader circles (e.g. recycling), because the energy and material leakages of the circuits are lower, and the value of the products is preserved. Additionally, the life of a product can be easily extended with little effort of repairing measures, while new production e.g. refurbishing or complete recycling is more complex (EMF, 2012).

2.2 Osterwalder's Business Model Canvas

"A business model describes the rationale of how an organization creates, delivers, and captures value" (Osterwalder & Pigneur, 2010, p. 15). Following Osterwalder

(2004), a BM can be described with nine Building Blocks (BB) that are visualized in **Fehler! Es wurde kein Textmarkenname vergeben.***Figure 3: The Nine Building Blocks (adopted from*: Osterwalder 2004). This visualization provides a concept of the most important parts that describe how a company conducts its business. The nine BBs can be separated into three dimensions. The Value Proposition consists of the value itself (products and services) and to whom (customer) the value is proposed. The second dimension is the value creation and delivery, which consists of four BB, the key partnerships, key activities, key resources and channels in order to deliver the value. The last dimension consists of the costs and revenues and explains how a company captures the value.

Value Proposition		Value Creation and Delivery		Value Capture
Value Proposition (Products and Services)		Key Partners		Cost Structure
		Key Activities	Key Resources	
Customer Segments	Customer Relationships	Channel		Revenue Stream

Figure 3: The Nine Building Blocks
(adopted from: Osterwalder 2004)

2.2.1 Value Proposition

The Value Proposition corresponds to the question of which value is provided and to whom it will be delivered. It encompasses all services and products of the company and the value a company offers to its customer. In other words, it shows how a company differentiates itself from its competitors. Another important feature of the Value Proposition is the target group and the kind of relationship a firm wants to establish with its customers. The BBs of the Value Proposition comprises the Value Proposition (VP), Customer Segments (CS), and Customer Relationships (CR) (Osterwalder & Pigneur, 2004).

8

Value Proposition (VP)
VP can be understood as the benefits delivered by the company to the customer (Bagchi & Tulskie, 2000). It is the overview of products and services that create the value for a CS. The VP is the bundle of products and services that a firm is offering and mainly the reason why customers buy from a certain firm.
Questions to find the VP: What is the product or service? or What value does the company offer to the market?
Customer Segments (CS)
CS are different groups of people a company is targeting. Selecting a firm's target customers is all about segmentation (Osterwalder & Pigneur, 2004). An effective segmentation leads to a target group that will be most attracted by your VP (Osterwalder & Pigneur, 2004). One of the most general distinction between target groups is, for example, the case of B2C (business-to-customer) and B2B (business-to-business).
Questions to find the CS: Who are the company's (target) customer? For whom are we creating value?
Customer Relationship (CR)
CR describe the different types of relationships between a company and its CS.
Questions to find the CR: How does the company build strong relationships? What type of relationship does our CS expect us to establish?

Table 1: Value Proposition
(based on: Osterwalder 2010)

2.2.2 Value Creation and Delivery

This section shows how a firm creates and delivers value to the customer. The BBs of this part are the Key Resources (KR), the Key Activities (KA), the Key Partnerships (KP), and finally the Channels (CH). The Value Creation encompasses all activities, resources, and partnerships that are crucial for a company to organize the production, infrastructure, and logistics. The Value Delivering can be described as the means and ways a firm gets in touch with its current and prospective customer to deliver created value (Osterwalder, 2004).

Key Resources (KR)
Most important assets required to make a BM work. The KR allow a company to create and offer the VP. KR can be categorized in physical, intellectual, human, and financial resources.
Questions to find the KR: What are the most important resources to organize production, infrastructure, and logistics and to offer the VP?
Key Activities (KA)
Actions that are most important to make the BM work. KA can be categorized in production, problem-solving, and platform/network.
Questions to find the KA: What are the most important activities to organize production, infrastructure, and logistics and to offer the VP?
Key Partnerships (KP)
A network of suppliers and partners that make the BM work. Companies create alliances to require resources, reduce risks, or optimize their BM. Partnerships can be created by three motivations: Optimization and economy of scale, reduction of risk and uncertainty, acquisition of particular resources and activities.
Questions to find the CH: Who are the most important partners to organize production, infrastructure, and logistics and what type of partnership is it?
Channels (CH)
The CH describes how a firm reaches and stays in contact with its (prospective) customers. The CH enables a firm to deliver a product or service to the customers, thus it is the connection between these two BBs. Osterwalder separates the channels in 5 phases, presented in the next line.

Awareness	Evaluation	Purchase	Delivery	After sales

Questions to find the CH: How does the company deliver the products or services to the CS?

Table 2: Value Creation and Delivery
(based on: Osterwalder 2010)

2.2.3 Value Capturing

The financials comprise the revenues and the costs, to capture the value of the BM.

Revenue Streams (R$)
The way a company generates cash from each CS
Questions to find the R$: How does the company create revenue?
Cost Structure (C$)
All costs incurred to operate a BM. Following Osterwalder, it is recommendable to distinguish between cost-driven and value-driven.
Questions to find the C$: What is the cost model for the VP?

Table 3: Value Capturing
(based on: Osterwalder 2010)

3 Cases

3.1 A Modular Mobile Phone

The first case in the analysis part is the "Fairphone 2". Fairphone started as a campaign for the non-profit organization Waag Society, which is a research institute in Amsterdam in 2013. The campaign wanted to reveal the bad working conditions in the production of smartphones in Asia and resource mining in Africa, which is an untransparent and dangerous business for the involved workers (Schmitt, 2013). After two and a half years as a campaign, they transformed into a start-up. They thought that if they were part of the economic system, they could implement better conditions in a more effective way. Bas van Abel, the founder of the company aims at finding a way to produce a "fair" and transparent mobile phone, especially focusing on the supply chain management (van Abel, 2018). The company names four principles on its website that should lead to this development: applying a long-lasting design, use of fair materials and resources, providing good working conditions in supplying companies in China and mining factories in Africa and South America, and reusing and recycling of materials (Fairphone, 2018). In 2013, the company launched the first edition of their phones financed via crowdsourcing (Schmitt, 2013). All together, they sold 60,000 "Fairphone 1" (Cuthbertson, 2016). Although their long-lasting design is one of their main goals, the company stopped selling the spare parts of modules to repair the Fairphone 1 in 2017 (Fairphone, 2017). In 2015, the company announced the Fairphone 2, which compared to the Fairphone 1, is a modular designed mobile phone (Fairphone, 2015). This edition is the first modular smartphone available for purchase and the first smartphone that is claimed to live for five years (Cuthbertson, 2015). The company strives to change the electronic industry from inside out by delivering a mobile phone that increases the awareness and demand for "fair" electronics and starts a conversation about more fairness amongst all involved players in the mobile phone industry (Fairphone, 2016). Regarding materials that are processed under fair working conditions and transparency in the supply chain, the company is a role model for the industry. The company wants to make their production completely transparent. Customer and consumer protectors can retrace where resources arise and which companies are involved in the production (von Lindern, 2014). But in the end, the company needs a running product. As an NGO, the company could spread the word, but now as a company, it requires a product with a message in order to remain competitive on the market (Schmitt, 2013).

3.2 A Refurbishment Service for Mobile Phones

The second case of the analysis part is "Mazuma Mobile", an online service platform, that focuses on collection or purchase, refurbishment or recycling, and the resale of mobile phones. The company was founded in 2006 by Charlo Carabott and John Lam and is based in Britain. In the mobile phone recycling/refurbishing industry, many companies offer cash for old electronic devices, and most of them go to global markets, such as in the Middle East, Africa, and South America. This is because such a BM is less expensive in the global south than in industrialized countries (Lunn, 2016).

In 2015, the company attracted much attention because Prince Charles of Wales spoke about Mazuma Mobile in his speech at Cambridge University about sustainable innovations in the UK. Prince Charles declared the company as an example of how companies should reduce waste and reconsider aspects of their supply chain (Prince Charles, 2015; Mazuma Mobile, 2018). Using the service of the company works as follows: Users that open the website face two possibilities. Either they can sell their old or broken mobile phones or buy a refurbished/reused one (Mazuma Mobile, n.d.). This business model, so-called "Recommerce", works as follows. The company acquires its products through collecting or buying them over their website. The amount of money that is paid to the product-owners depends on the quality of the old mobile phones. (Hahler & Fleischmann, 2017). When the old mobile phone arrives at the company, it is either directly reused or repaired. In the case that the device is not repairable, it is being recycled. Regarding the payments to the customers, the industry faces different problems. Recycling companies are criticized because of requoting deceits. This requoting means that after sending the mobile phone to the company, they change the original offer. The most common reason for requoting is when someone sells a faulty device as working. The customer then has to pay back the shipping, which is sometimes even more than the price. Mazuma Mobile says that they distinguish between faulty devices and mobile phones that have scratches and scuffs but in the case of the company changing the offer, the user can get back his mobile phone for free (Lunn, 2016).

4 Analysis

In this chapter, we conduct a case study of two BMs. We will analyze the BMs of Fairphone and Mazuma Mobile based on Osterwalder's Business Model Canvas. The analysis is to detect the crucial building blocks that stand out and show how the cases correspond to the idea, concepts, and principles of the CE.

4.1 Methodology

Case studies are not only used to describe a unit of analysis but also as a research method. In the exploratory phase of a research topic, a case study research is useful to discover facts and issues about a topic. It can not only be used in an **exploratory** way but also in an **explanatory** way to test, develop, or even compare theories. Case study research aims at comprehending "how" and "why" a business works. By studying the subject matter in context, multiple sources of evidence are used, coming from interviews and articles in newspapers and documents on the websites. We derived most of our information about the companies from blogs they provide as information on the internet. So, the case study is conducted by electronic documents, interviews, and press articles. There are three important points about the definition of a case study. First, case study research always involves a company. Second, it does not involve fieldwork or participant observation. And third, in order to reach valuable outcomes, case study research is philosophically neutral. That means it can be conducted according to positive, interpretive, or critical tenets (Myers, 2013). We will first use the case study in an exploratory way, to find out the BM of the cases. Later, in the discussion the case study will be used in an explanatory way, to compare the BMs of the cases. Business models have become a new unit to analyze the business logic of a firm (Stähler, 2002). The research approach was taken from Osterwalder who argues that BMs can improve measuring, observing, and comparing the business logic of a firm (Osterwalder et al., 2005). The business model is largely observable and can be copied from outside of a person (Teece, 2010). Osterwalder's clearly arranged overview is one of the most common conceptualizations of BMs. With the help of Osterwalder's Canvas, we will allocate the crucial information about every BB. The information is mostly based on information given by the companies through their website. The financial situation of the companies will not be intensively analyzed by the Canvas of Osterwalder. We will just give a quick overview of where the costs and revenues come from. This stems from the fact that the costs of the cases, as well as the revenues, are (yet) not able to be discussed in the context of the CE. This will be explained more detailed in the limitations.

4.2 The Business Model of Fairphone

In the following, the BM of Fairphone will be explained. First, we will analyze which value is provided and to whom in *Table 4: The Value Proposition of Fairphone*. Second, we will focus on how the value is provided in *Table 5: The Value Creation and Delivery of Fairphone*. Finally, we will take a quick look on the value capturing, before the Nine Building Blocks of Fairphone will be presented all together in *Figure 4: The Nine Building Blocks of Fairphone*

(adopted from: Osterwalder 2004).

Value Proposition	Customer Segments	Customer Relationships
"Fair" Mobile Phone Modular Product Design Co-Creation	Conscious Customer	Self-Service

Table 4: The Value Proposition of Fairphone

The core value of Fairphone's BM is that the company aims at producing and delivering a "fair" phone. Nevertheless, the company is (yet) not able to produce a phone that is 100 percent fair. The company is also not able to describe the "fair" way of production in the mobile phone industry. However, this is not their goal. By making the value chain transparent, the company started and still guides the conversation about the moral issues surrounding the mobile phone industry. The company's customers buy their products because of their vision and the anticipated change of the industry from within (Wernink & Strahl, 2015). As already mentioned, the company has four principles that describe and differentiate it from other smartphones (Fairphone, 2018). The long-lasting **design** is the most important and implemented one. The company based the product design of the Fairphone 2 on modularity. This modularity supports repairability without specific expertise or tools (van Abel, 2018). If the screen is broken, customers can order another one on the website and replace it by themselves. The spare parts can be new or refurbished ones. The company guarantees, that the quality and optic does not differ between a refurbished and a new one (Fairphone, 2019). The company makes it easy for customers to repair the phone and use it longer. Instructions to repair specific modules can be accessed on their website as video sequences. Additionally, the company partnered with "iFixit" to make the repairing process easier for every customer (Wernink & Strahl, 2015). "iFixit" provides the described repair instructions on their website. These self-repairing possibilities lead to longer use because the user does not need to order a new phone, due to a broken camera. The company wants to extend the longevity of a smartphone from two to five years. The idea behind this is that the customers use their phones twice as long as e.g. an iPhone user. Consequently, only half of the phones need to be produced and thus also half of the resources are needed (van Abel, 2018; van der Velden, 2016). Following van Abel's argument, the effect of this long-lasting design will be less waste and less production. In the end, this is more sustainable because the industry does not plan in five-year cycles. This means that companies do not plan on their customers to use a phone for five years (van Abel, 2018).

Another benefit of the modularity is the **customization** possibility. The Fairphone 2 possesses an extension port. New technologies or modules can be integrated, such as near-field communication (NFC) (Cuthbertson, 2015). Wireless charging and a case with solar panels were considered for use, but not yet implemented (Cuthbertson, 2015). The company is also planning to provide improved camera modules and third-party manufacturers may also develop their own implemented camera modules (Cuthbertson, 2015).

The company's **Customer Segments (CS)** consist mainly of people who are convinced by the idea and the project of the firm (von Lindern, 2016). Their customers are aware of the situation in the mobile phone industry and want a production that is fair, instead of technological newness. The most important and biggest market for Fairphone is Germany. The company sold around 36.000 devices (Brodersen, 2018). They aim at increasing the number of customers by providing more transparency in their production process. Increasing the number of customers leads to an increasing demand and - following the company's logic - the industry then has to produce more sustainable and offer products that are more sustainable (Wernink & Strahl, 2015).

One part of the **Customer Relationship (CR)** is based on self-service. Regarding the repairing possibilities, customers can find any information to repair a broken screen on the website. The company maintains no direct relationship with the customer, that means the customer does not need personal assistance. Nevertheless, the company wants their customers to co-create value by providing open-source hardware and software. This means that everyone can develop parts of the software. Van Abel sees Fairphone as a platform for everybody (companies, consumer, and programmer) to think about sustainability (van Abel, 2018). The company's vision is to create a community of people who want to deal with the moral issues surrounding the mobile phone industry. Customers, supporters, or followers can share their thoughts and ideas under #WeAreFairphone on social media (Wernink & Strahl, 2015). This growing movement is part of Fairphone's vision. The company sees itself on a journey towards a fair economy (Wernink & Strahl, 2015).

Key Partnerships	Key Activities	Key Resources	Chan-nels
Mining factories Manufacturer	Production Supply Chain Management	Intellectual Website	Online

Table 5: The Value Creation and Delivery of Fairphone

This section shows how the company creates and delivers its VP. As we already know the value creation is crucial in order to organize the production.

The **Key Resources (KR)** the company needs for its products arise from intellectual and human kind. Intellectual resources such as brands, partnerships, and knowledge are important components of the BM. Human resources are crucial because of the creative innovative part that is responsible for the design and development of the mobile phone.

The **Key Activity (KA)** of Fairphone is obviously the production of the VP, the "fair" phone. A fair supply chain management is the first KA. Recycling is the second KA. This way of production is supposed to lead to a long-lasting design. The Fairphone 2 contains 40 different elements from all around the world (Fairphone, 2017). It is obvious that this global way of production leads to a very complex and non-transparent supply chain. As already mentioned, a campaign of the Dutch Waag Society about conflict minerals in eastern Congo was the starting point of the Fairphone project. They showed the involvement of the mining industry in the civil war, child labor and how it finances warlords (Schmitt, 2013). The non-transparent supply chains in the mobile phone industry are one of the problems that Fairphone tries to solve. One cannot trace back the minerals to where they come from after they have been delivered to various ports in the Indian Ocean. Afterward, minerals are shipped to smelting factories in eastern Asia, before a company manufactures the electronic device (Schmitt, 2013). With the increasing attention on the conflict minerals, the US introduced with the Dott-Frank Act, a provision for companies that examine their supply chains for conflict minerals (Seay, 2012). In contrast to other companies that reacted to the Dott-Frank Act and the increasing public pressure by purchasing conflict minerals from Australia, Fairphone knew this would not change the situation of African miners (van Abel, 2018). Fairphone still buys in the Democratic Republic of Congo, but they are cooperating with different initiatives to improve the working conditions and facilitate the tracking and tracing of minerals (van Abel, 2018). Tin, tantalum (cobalt), tungsten, and gold are the most commonly mined conflict minerals also known as "3TG" and four of the 40 elements in the Fairphone 2 (Schmitt, 2013). In the case of tin, which is mined in the Democratic Republic of Congo (DRC) and used for soldering the components, Fairphone works together with the Conflict-free Tin Initiative (Fairphone, 2017). Regarding tantalum (coltan), which is used to produce capacitors on the circuit board of the Fairphone 2, they cooperate with "Solutions for Hope". The Fairphone 2 is now produced with conflict-free tantalum from the DRC (Fairphone, 2017). In order to produce the vibration motors with tungsten in a transparent way, Fairphone collaborated with an Austrian smelter to reopen the trade in Rwanda (Fairphone, 2017). Additionally, the company achieved the very first fair-trade gold supply chain from Peru with assistance from Fairtrade (Fairphone, 2017). As part of Fairphone's production and one of the KA, Fairphone seeks to increase the global supply and demand for recycled materials by promoting recycling and encouraging suppliers to use recycled materials (Fairphone, 2016). The company created a plastic case for their phone that consists of 65 percent recycled plastic and used recycled copper for the circuit board of the phone (van der Velden, 2016; Fairphone, 2016). Together with the Initiative "Closing the Loop", the company developed a sustainable solution for e-waste in countries without officially regulated recycling sectors. In Ghana, this alliance collected 75,000 discarded phones and shipped it to a proper recycling plant in Belgium. The company itself says on their website:

> "Based on currently available recycling methods, (...) disassembling the phone before recycling would lead to the greatest amount of recovered materials. Modularity makes our phones easier to disassemble, but the best-case scenario still only recovers around one third of the original materials"

(Fairphone, 2017).

In November 2014, the company started a recycling program in Europe together with "Teqcycle". The program calls on the public to donate their old cell phones and guarantees safe recycling and the avoidance of landfills. Broken phones are recycled and working devices are reused. Used and faulty modules can also be sent back to the company, to repair or recycle them (Fairphone, 2016). HI-P is Fairphone's production partner in China. The company made some tangible improvements regarding fire safety measures, better safety clothing, and even structural changes like lesser working hours in order to guarantee Fairphone's VP, the promise of a fair production (Fairphone, 2016). They also introduced a social fund for the well-being of workers which means that for every phone that is sold, both companies pay into the fund, to better meet the worker's need and to support their training and development (Fairphone, 2016).

The acquisition of resources and activities can be described as the way the company creates its **Key Partnerships (KP)**. The production of the phone is completely outsourced. The company's KP to supply the VP needs to encompass the relationships with the African suppliers of the raw materials, the initiatives which assess, improve, and organize the supply chain to the manufacturers and the Asian manufacturers.

Solutions for Hope	Conflict-free tantalum (coltan) from DRC
Conflict-free tin Initiative	Conflict-free tin from DRC
Closing the Loop	Solutions for E-waste
iFixit	Provide open-source reparation
Hi-P	Asian manufacturer
Teqcycle	Donation program for old mobile phones

Table 6: The Key Partnerships and shared Projects of Fairphone

Customers can order the Fairphone 2 and all components to repair the phone on the company's website. This is the most important **Channel (CH)** for the company. They service a blog with current information about the projects and efforts. The company has many online partners, who are also offering their phones (Mobilcom-Debitel, Klarmobil, Edeka, Otto, Memo, and Vireo). Only a few of these partners, e.g. Telekom in Austria, are however selling the phones in stores (von Lindern, 2016; Brodersen, 2018). The company still plans to distribute the mobile phones via Telekom Germany, who is supporting the project, Telekom helped them with certification issues (Brodersen, 2018).

Awareness:	Evaluation:	Purchase:	Delivery:	After Sales:
Internet/Blog Word-of-Mouth	Blog on the Website	Website Online Retailer	Post	E-Mail, Blog, Community Member

Table 7: The Channel Phases of Fairphone
(based on: Osterwalder 2010)

The company captures the value of the BM through a **Revenue Stream (R$)** generated by sales of the long-life product. Buying a Fairphone 2 in January 2019 thus costs 399€ while the original price was 529€.

Fairphone is completely transparent about the **Cost Structure (C$)**, to give the customer a detailed overview, where their money goes (Fairphone, 2016; van der Velden, 2016). The complete costs are listed on the company's website.

Value Proposition	Value Creation and Delivery		Value Capture
"Fair" Mobile Phone Modular Product Design Co-Creation	Mining factories Manufacturing companies		Value-driven
	Supply Chain Management Production	Intellectual Website	
Conscious Customer	Self-Service	Online Website	Asset Sale

Figure 4: The Nine Building Blocks of Fairphone
(adopted from: Osterwalder 2004)

4.3 The Business Model of Mazuma Mobile

In the following, the BM of Mazuma Mobile will be explained. First, we will analyze which value is provided and to whom in *Table 8: The Value Proposition of Mazuma Mobile.* Second, we will focus on how the value is provided in *Table 9: The Value Creation and Delivery of Mazuma Mobile.* Finally, we will take a quick look on the value capturing, before the Nine Building Blocks of Mazuma Mobile will be presented all together in *Figure 5: The Nine Building Blocks of Mazuma Mobile*

(adopted from: Osterwalder 2004).

Value Proposition	Customer Relationships	Customer Segments
Recommerce Make money out of your old mobile phone Recycling Refurbished smartphones	Everything is made to be as easy as possible	Multi-sided platforms People with broken/unused mobile phones People with demand for technology for little cash

Table 8: The Value Proposition of Mazuma Mobile

The VP of Mazuma Mobile consists of several parts. First, customers can buy refurbished smartphones for a low price. Second, they can make money out of their old,
or broken mobile phones. As already mentioned, the company provides an online
service platform to collect (through purchasing) old/broken phones. These phones
are recycled or refurbished and sold (in order to reuse the mobile phones). The
company provides a platform for users to sell and buy mobile phones, tablets, or
smartwatches. In order to sell an old mobile phone, the user must give information
about the mobile phone model, whether it is working or faulty and choose the pay-
ment method. Eventually, the company proposes a guaranteed value, also known
as a fixed price which is requoted in only 6 percent of devices (Lunn, 2016). If the
user accepts the offer, he receives a little bag for free to send off the mobile phone.
If everything is in order, the user will receive the money on the same day, the phone
arrives at the company. Another reason to use the service of Mazuma Mobile besides a modest sum for the old mobile phone is the fact that it is an easy way to get
rid of the toxic materials the phones contain (Mazuma Mobile, 2012). After sending
the mobile phone to the company, they can directly reuse and sell the collected mobile phone, given the fact that the phone is still working. In case the phone needs
refurbishment, the company ships it to their partner repair centers. The company
complains that the large majority (around 90 percent) of an average 150,000
phones they receive every month, can be reused and the demand for secondhand
mobile phones continues to grow in the UK (Mazuma Mobile, 2018). Obsolete or
completely broken phones are excluded from refurbishing, the company however
still accepts them at no cost and makes sure they are recycled. So, if a customer
does not want to hold the device at home, neither bring it to a recycling company,
giving it to Mazuma Mobile is a convenient way to get rid of their old mobile phones
and sometimes even getting some money back (EMF, 2011).

Even though the company's headquarters are in Britain, they have branches all over
the world, especially in countries of the Global South like India, China, and Brazil.
They profit off the fact that the markets with the highest demand of a model offer
the highest prices for it. With the help of external partners (phone retailer, insurance companies, repair centers) with whom they established long-term relationships, the devices are then refurbished and redistributed (Mazuma Mobile, 2018).
This means that selling to the market with the highest demand leads to the highest
price, the company can get for an old model. This can be described as the VP for
users of Mazuma Mobile. Making money out of their old mobile phones. The other
service provided by the company is that customers can buy a refurbished mobile

phone for a low price. Sometimes there is no difference between a new phone or a refurbished one, in case the mobile phone only has a small damage, e.g. a broken screen or a damaged button. The repairing is not complicated, and the profit can be higher for the company (Mazuma Mobile, 2018).

The company distinguishes their customers in two **Customer Segments (CS)** which means that the company is a "multi-sided platform". The first CS includes everyone with a broken or unused mobile phone. The so-called "sell-users" are the ones who deliver the resources for the company. These customers must trust the company, in order to maintain a long-term relationship. People usually possess more than one phone in their lives, which explains why the company is so interested in receiving the old and unused phones of their customers. The "buy-user" is someone who needs or wants a technological device but has less access to capital or does not feel the need to obtain a new one.

The **Customer Relationships (CR)** of the company take place mostly on the website of the company. First, the company wants to provide a stress-free customer experience for every CS in order to build a strong long-term relationship. The company made the whole process as easy as possible. Starting with figuring out the value of the old/broken mobile phone, to the delivery of it, the company implemented a system that seeks to be transparent and simple. If there occur still complications, customers are able to contact the company via online chat on the website. The company assumes that this service and availability is expected by the CSs. When buying a refurbished mobile phone (even for little money) it should work without complicated contractual or financial details. The company's service - for the mobile phone that they sell - includes free returns within fourteen days and a full refund, a twelve months warranty and free delivery (Mazuma Mobile, n.d.).

Key Partnerships	Key Activities	Key Resources	Channels
Repairing/recycling companies in the UK and in other countries	Collection Reverse logistics Estimating the value of the device	Old mobile phones trade-in website	Website mazumamobile.com

Table 9: The Value Creation and Delivery of Mazuma Mobile

This section explains, how the company creates and then delivers its VP. The company requires different activities, resources, and partnerships to provide the VP. The first **Key Activity (KA)** for the company is to collect the KR, in this case: old mobile phones. Therefore, the company organizes the reverse logistics by providing the tools for trade-in programs, collection containers and arrangements of the shipping. On their website, the company provides the possibility for customers to sell their mobile phones. With the information about the phone's model and whether it is faulty or working, the company estimates and offers a price. For this purpose, the company accesses a database containing a continuously updated list of models and their prices depending on their condition. This database, as well as the website, are one of the **Key Resources (KR)**. The company can also check whether the phone is lost or stolen with the help of insurance companies that co-operate with them. If the customer accepts the offer, he receives a bag and sends the device to the company. After Mazuma Mobile receives the bag, an on-site WEEE (Waste Electrical and Electronic Equipment) treatment facility tests and categorizes the mobile phone (Mazuma Mobile, 2018). This facility decides whether the device goes to a reuse partner or will be recycled by a recycling partner. The reuse partner will either clean, polish or repair the mobile phone. The recycling partner will recycle the phones.

The company has many **Key Partnerships (KP)** including mobile phone retailers, repair centers and insurance companies to make the BM work. As already mentioned, due to the export of particular devices, the company has partners overseas, with whom they keep long-term relationships as well. The company also cooperates with phone retailers because they do not sell all mobile phones on their website. Insurance companies are also clients. When their customers lose a phone, or it is stolen, they get a replacement-phone provided by Mazuma Mobile.

The owned **Channel (CH)** provided by the company in order to deliver the VP is the website "mazumamobile.com", and it is also the most important CH. The process of buying back from customers and selling the refurbished mobile phones is carried out on the website. The website represents a platform of trade, it is the company's trade-in. The CH serve several functions that are presented in.

Raise Awareness:	Website and Internet
Help to Evaluate:	Chat and Website
Allow Purchase:	Website
Delivery:	Post and own bags
Provide After Sales:	Chat, website and mailing list

Table 10: The Channel Phases of Mazuma Mobile

The value captured by the BM is based on **Revenue Streams (R$)** from selling the refurbished mobile phones and from material recycling. Of course, the value of the mobile phones depends on the model, their condition and age.

The **Cost Structure (C$)** encompasses the purchasing of old mobile phones and their repairing and refurbishment. Servicing the website belongs to another important cost in order to deliver the KR and KA.

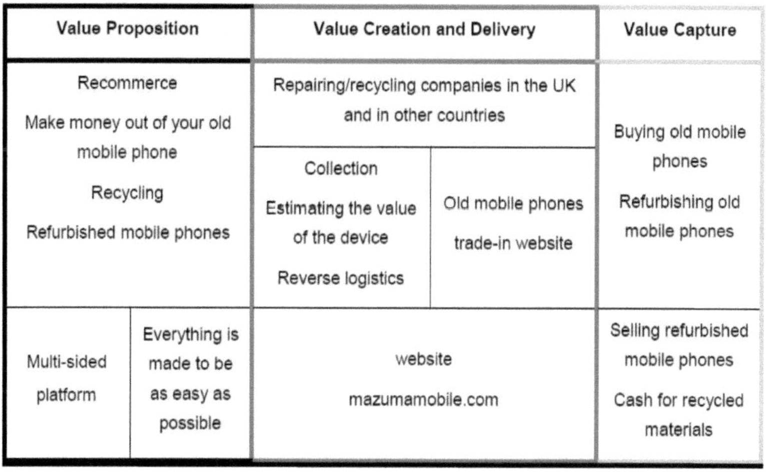

Value Proposition		Value Creation and Delivery		Value Capture
Recommerce Make money out of your old mobile phone Recycling Refurbished mobile phones		Repairing/recycling companies in the UK and in other countries		Buying old mobile phones Refurbishing old mobile phones
		Collection Estimating the value of the device Reverse logistics	Old mobile phones trade-in website	
Multi-sided platform	Everything is made to be as easy as possible	website mazumamobile.com		Selling refurbished mobile phones Cash for recycled materials

Figure 5: The Nine Building Blocks of Mazuma Mobile (adopted from: Osterwalder 2004)

5 Discussion

This case-study-based analysis allows us to reflect on the role of two companies in the mobile phone industry. In the last chapter, we analyzed the cases, in this chapter we want to interpret and discuss how the BMs correspond to the CE and which principles of the CE are implemented. Six key factors were extracted in the theoretical foundation: the principles of the Technical Cycle of the CE (Maintain, Reuse, Refurbish, Recycle), the principles that originate from the three R's (Reduction, Reuse, Recycle) and the principle of Design. Both cases will be taken into consideration and we will analyze to what extent these principles are followed. Finally, we want to explain which limitations we faced and give some theoretical and practical implications.

5.1 Fairphone and Mazuma Mobile in the Context of the Circular Economy

Generally, it can be said, that the value of a classical long-life product is to create and deliver a durable product. Therefore, the Fairphone 2 is categorized as a "classical long-life" model (Bakker et al., 2014). Due to its **modular design**, the Fairphone 2 is made for multiple cycles of use which leads to a prolonged life of the product. If a specific module of the hardware is not working anymore, it can be fixed instead of changing the complete device. The Fairphone 2 can even be reused if components are broken, whilst for classical phones, this would mean that they have to be thrown away or need to be repaired by the company, which takes a lot of time. The modularity of the product is created to be easily repairable and maintainable, which leads not only to prolonged life but also to prolonged use of the product with less creation of electronic waste and more possibilities of reuse (Schneider et al., 2018; Van den Berg & Bakker, 2015). However, modularity is not the most sustainable option because it can lead to a rebound effect and even more consumption (Schischke et al., 2016). Regarding Reduction, Fairphone sends the products without charger and headphones. The customer only receives the electronic device because Fairphone assumes that everybody possesses a classical charger for smartphones. Reflecting Figure 2: The Technical Cycle of the Circular Economy (adopted from: EMF 2012). we can infer that the company has implemented the CE in its BM in several ways. Regarding **Maintaining**, the company has made the self-repairing possibilities and the co-creation as one of the VP and it is the basis of the CR. As long as the user possesses the product, he himself can repair it and maintenance is given. The company wants their customers to use the phone at least five years and using the modular design, they created a way to do so. The maintaining principle seems to be implemented in a way, that Fairphone's customers are able to maintain their phone. The **Reuse** principle is applied in a way that used modules as well as the complete mobile phones can be sent back to the company. Depending on the condition, the company reuses, repairs or recycles it. Fairphone considers **Refurbishment** in case the returning modules are faulty but repairable. Therefore, the company has created partnerships. The refurbishing partner takes care of the repairing and delivers the module back to the company so they can send it back to customers. The recycling partner recycles the devices in order to not throw away the materials. Even though Fairphone provides **recycling** activities, they found, that only one-third of the original materials of the Fairphone 2 could be recycled. The goal is that the company uses the resources "mined" from recycled phones for the production of new devices. This would be effectively closing the loop in the supply chain and is likely to be a mass balance system. To reach this Fairphone should cooperate with recycling partners who sell only recycled materials on the market (Wernink & Strahl, 2015). Figure 6 provides a picture of the activities of Fairphone in the CE. One CE-loops is directly addressed through the company: Maintaining. The other loops are indirectly addressed by the company, due to the fact that they are provided by partner companies. These loops include 1) Reuse, 2) Refurbish and 3) Recycle.

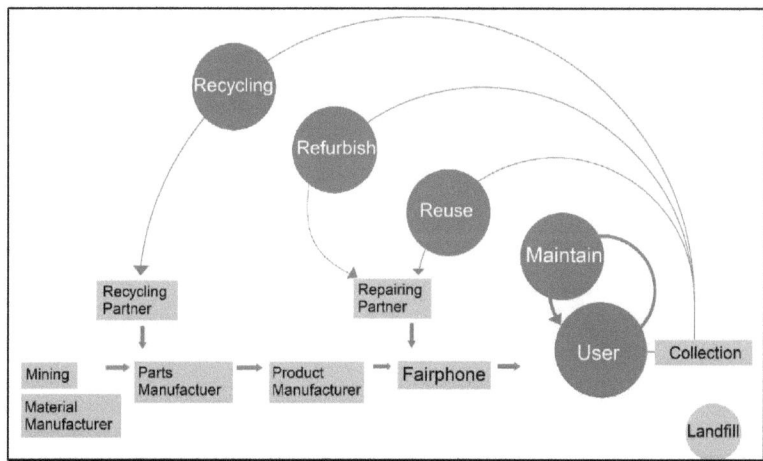

Figure 6: Fairphone in the Circular Economy
(adopted from: EMF 2015)

In the following, we will discuss Mazuma Mobile in the context of the circular economy. Generally, the VP of a gap-exploiter model is a service or product that is based on the exploitation of left-over product value in a system, for example, repairing, refurbishing or recycling. Therefore, we call Mazuma Mobile a "gap-exploiter" model (Bakker et al., 2014). Going back to Figure 2: The Technical Cycle of the Circular Economy (adopted from: EMF 2012)., we will now assess how the company applied the principles of CE. Regarding the principle of **maintaining**, it could be assumed that the company follows the principle because the life of the mobile phone is prolonged. However, it should be differentiated between the action of the company and the user. Since the user is responsible for maintaining the mobile phone, the company only provides the reuse, refurbishment, and recycling. The company's BM is thus rather focused on **reusing**. Mobile phones in a condition that only requires cleaning and other cosmetic repairs are prepared for reuse by a repairing partner and then sold by the company or another second-hand mobile phone retailer. Mobile phones that require **refurbishing**, which means mobile phones with minor hardware defects (e.g. battery, scratches, screen, etc.), are refurbished by repairing partners. Through the refurbishment of old devices, there is less production of new devices and less mining of resources. In order to provide **recycling** activities, the company has created partnerships. Only mobile phones with major hardware defects will be recycled. The recycled mobile phones and their resources stay in the circle and are not thrown away. Mazuma Mobile does not provide information on whether the recycled resources are used to produce mobile phones or something else. Regarding **Reduction**, Mazuma Mobile is a company that reduces the demand to produce new electronic devices, while increasing the demand for second-hand electronics. Figure 7 provides a picture of the activities of Mazuma Mobile in the CE. The "Maintaining Circle" and the "Product Manufacturer" are left out due to the fact, that both do not exist in the BM of the company.

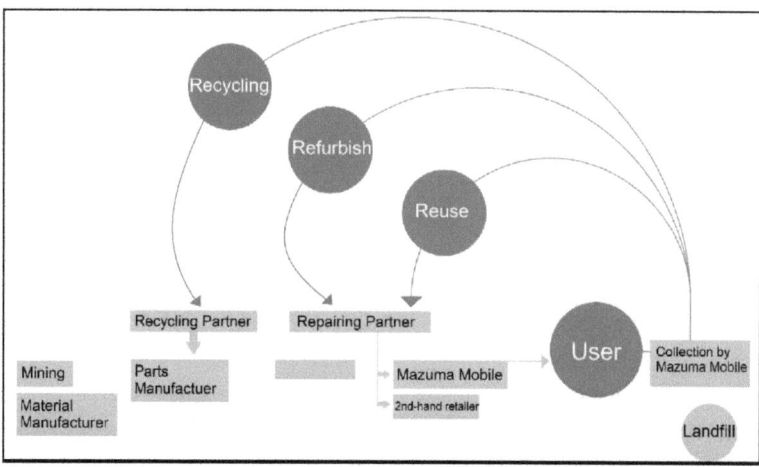

Figure 7: Mazuma Mobile in the Circular Economy
(adopted from: EMF 2015)

To conclude the discussion, it can be said that both BM's meet some of the require-
ments of the CE. Fairphone as a classical long-live product that found amazing ways
to implement principles of the CE. Mazuma Mobile is a gap-exploiting service that
recycles just a few of its collecting devices, while around 90 percent of the collected
phones will be reused after refurbishing or repairing. This means that both companies are trying to slow down the resource loops. Fairphone is designed for long use
and Mazuma Mobile extends the life of mobile phones. Regarding Fairphone, it can
be observed that the loops become more relevant from the outside to the inside.
This means a mobile phone first requires some maintenance and then repairs or
exchange. Even though the possibility of repairing the Fairphone poses an ad-
vantage compared to other phones, it is obvious that it would be even better if the
device did not break at all in order to maximize the lifetime. Mazuma Mobile, on
the other hand, focuses mostly on reusing and refurbishing electric devices but do
not implement any maintaining activities aimed at affecting the customer's behav-
ior of consumption. The discussion showed that it is difficult whether one BM corresponds better to the idea of the CE than the other. Both companies still have to
fill a lot of gaps in order to claim to be a circular BM. One thing can be said though:
if the mobile phone industry would work like Fairphone and prolong the use of
mobile phones, Business Models such as Mazuma Mobile could not exist anymore.
Since there are millions of unused mobile phones though, Mazuma Mobile is a very
important part of the development directing to the CE.

5.2 Implications for Theory and Practice

The results showed that the promotion of consumer responsibility is crucial, but still not well implemented (Ghisellini, Cialani, & Ulgiati, 2016). Mazuma Mobile only motivates consumers to offer old mobile phones but not to maintain their use. It has also been shown that circular supply chains mostly consider the production and distribution but not the consumption processes (Lieder & Rashid, 2016). In practice, the results regarding Fairphone implicate that the main factors for purchase are the values and norms underlying the company. To deeper implement the principles of the CE, Fairphone should invest in their partnerships concerning recycling and refurbishing. Fairphone should also investigate in product-service systems since they already planned to implement it and many researchers found the positive correlation between CE and product-service systems (Lewandowski, 2016). Regarding Mazuma Mobile, the future predicts a growing second-hand mobile phone industry. Therefore, the BMs acting in this industry will have to better organize the take-back processes, e.g. through an engagement with telecommunication providers. New mobile phones could also be linked to a buy-back option. Therefore, closer collaborations between retailers and network providers are necessary.

Further research questions would be how Fairphone implemented the product-service systems and how it led to the developments they desire. Another important research topic is the circular and modular design. However, this should start at the level of the parts manufacturer and thus become an industry-wide standard.

5.3 Limitations

Even though this study aims at analyzing two BMs in the context of the CE, there are some limitations. Further research should cover all details of the Business Model Canvas in the context of the CE. However, 100 percent circular BM do not (yet) exist, because it is impossible to create no waste at all (this has physical and practical reasons) (Van Renswoude et al., 2015). Moreover, there is no generally accepted circular BM with whom the cases could be compared. The financials are not considered in the analysis and discussing them in the context of the CE has been skipped because following Lewandowski (2015), revenues and costs in the CE should mostly be associated with the product-service-system and "Fairphone" only planned to implement a product-service system (customer pays a periodic fee for getting the access of using), and Mazuma Mobile provides selling products as well.

6 Conclusion

This thesis sought to analyze two Business Models in the mobile phone industry in the context of the Circular Economy. The motivation of this bachelor thesis was to acknowledge the problems that crop up due to the way of production in the mobile phone industry. Electronic devices are irreplaceable in our lives and still, most of the people are not aware of these conflicts and issues arising because of our demand for cheap technology. There are problems concerning the mining of raw materials in the DRC, which are crucial for the production of smartphones, the activities around the manufacturing of the smartphone in China and the environmental problems caused by the production. All these issues resulted in the realization that there is a need for change in the industry to ameliorate the situation. The objective of this study was not to solve these problems but to reflect on the role of Fairphone and Mazuma Mobile in this industry. First, we pointed out the Circular Economy and its principles around the three R's (Reduce, Reuse, Recycle), the Technical Cycle of the Circular Economy that adds the principles of Maintaining and Refurbishing and the crucial principle of Design. Even though there is no clear definition of the CE, it still gives a direction for the economy that can be associated with sustainable developments. The Circular Economy is getting more and more recognition in research and practice. Many companies are striving to implement some of the principles. The importance of this study lies in providing a good overview of the Circular Economy, in order to find the crucial elements of the Business Models. They play an important role in this development since they are the rationale of how a company creates, delivers and captures value. For this topic, we used Osterwalder's Canvas. The Nine Building Blocks provide a clear overview and a structured analysis of the cases. The case study has allowed us to reflect on the Business Models of Fairphone and Mazuma Mobile. Therefore, we focused on the Value Proposition and the Value Creation. The Value Delivering and Value Capturing has been noticed, but finally excluded from the discussion. This has been done due to the fact that only the Value Proposition and Creation of the cases affect the principles of the CE. It became clear that despite their name, Fairphone is not producing fair phones. It is a classical long-live product, that implemented all the principles mentioned in the theory. Some of the principles are implemented in a poor way and definitely need improvement. Nevertheless, Fairphone wants to start a discussion about the definition of fair and develop best practices. It is a long way that Fairphone wants to go in the hope of creating a truly ethical smartphone, but it can change the industry, piece by piece. The main results regarding Mazuma Mobile were that their gap-exploiting service is crucial for increasing development of the industry in a circular direction. Even if they did not implement the principle of maintaining, Mazuma Mobile reveals a lack in the industry and makes people think about their consumption.

All in all, it can be said that the increasing success of both companies lead to a more innovative industry and a better implementation of the principles of the Circular Economy gives the hope that one day we can say that the mobile phone industry is not the excessive one from today. 124 million unused mobile phones in Germany are 124 million mobile phones too many and both companies are working towards the reduction of this number.

References

Bagchi, S., & Tulskie, B. (2000). E-business models: integrating learning from strategy development experiences and empirical research. *20th Annual International Conference of the Strategic Management Society*, (pp. 15-18).

Bakker, C., den Hollander, M., Van Hinte, E., & Zljlstra, Y. (2014). *Products that last: Product design for circular business models.* TU Delft Library.

Bakker, C., Wang, F., Huisman, J., & den Hollander, M. (2014). Products that go round: exploring product life extension through design. *Journal of Cleaner Production, 69*, pp. 10-16.

Bitkom. (2018). *124 Millionen Alt-Handys liegen ungenutzt herum.* Retrieved 4. December, 2018, from https://www.bitkom.org/Presse/Presseinformation/124-Millionen-Alt-Handys-liegen-ungenutzt-herum.html

Boons, F., & Lüdeke-Freund, F. (2013). Business models for sustainable innovation: state-of-the-art and steps towards a research agenda. *Journal of Cleaner production, 45*, pp. 9-19.

Boulding, K. (1966). *The economics of the coming spaceship earth. Environmental Quality Issues in a Growing Economy.*

Brodersen, B. (2018). *Telekom: Fairphone-Verkauf ist nicht vom Tisch.* Retrieved 5. January, 2019, from http://www.areamobile.de/news/48309-telekom-fairphone-verkauf-ist-nicht-vom-tisch

Brown, B., Hanson, M., Liverman, D., & Merideth, R. (1987). Global sustainability: toward definition. *Environmental management, 11(6)*, pp. 713-719.

Campagnolo, D., & Camuffo, A. (2010). The concept of modularity in management studies: a literature review. *International journal of management reviews, 12(3)*, pp. 259-283.

Castellani, V., Sala, S., & Mirabella, N. (2015). Beyond the throwaway society: A life cycle-based assessment of the environmental benefit of reuse. *Integrated environmental assessment and management, 11(3)*, pp. 373-382.

Cuthbertson, A. (2015). *Fairphone 2: World's first modular smartphone is revolutionising electronics piece by piece.* Retrieved 20. December, 2018, from https://www.ibtimes.co.uk/fairphone-2-worlds-first-modular-smartphone-revolutionising-electronics-piece-by-piece-1526141

Cuthbertson, A. (2016). *Fairphone 2 review: the world's first modular smartphone will last you for years.* Retrieved 21. December, 2018, from https://www.newsweek.com/fairphone-2-review-414702

Deutsche Umwelthilfe. (2018). *Nachhaltigkeit von Geschäftsmodellen in der Informations- und Kommunikationstechnik.* Retrieved December 10. January, 2018, from https://www.duh.de/fileadmin/user_upload/download/Projektinformati on/Kreislaufwirtschaft/Elektroger%C3%A4te/180115_DUH-Studie_Nachhaltigkeit-IKT-Industrie.pdf

Dießenbacher, J., & Reller, A. (2016). *"Das 'Fairphone' – ein Impuls in Richtung nachhaltige Elektronik?".* Berlin: Springer Spektrum.

EMF. (2011). Retrieved 1. December, 2018, from Collection, refurbishment and resale of mobile phone handsets: https://www.ellenmacarthurfoundation.org/case-studies/collection-refurbishment-and-resale-of-mobile-phone-handsets

EMF. (2012). *Towards the Circular Economy 1. Economic and Business Rationale for an Accelerated Transition. Ellen MacArthur Foundation.* Retrieved 4. December, 2018, from https://www.ellenmacarthurfoundation.org/assets/downloads/publicati ons/Ellen-MacArthur-Foundation-Towards-the-Circular-Economy-vol.1.pdf

EMF. (2015). *Delivering the circular economy: A toolkit for policymakers.* Retrieved 2. December, 2018, from https://www.ellenmacarthurfoundation.org/assets/downloads/publicati ons/EllenMacArthurFoundation_PolicymakerToolkit.pdf

EMF. (2015). *Towards a circular economy - Business rationale for an accelerated transition.* Retrieved 4. December, 2018, from https://www.ellenmacarthurfoundation.org/assets/downloads/TCE_Elle n-MacArthur-Foundation_9-Dec-2015.pdf

EU. (2008). *Directive 2008/98/EC of the European Parliament and of the Council of 19 november 2008 on waste and repealing certain directives.* Official Journal of EU, L 312, 19.11.2008. Retrieved 2. December, 2018, from https://eur-lex.europa.eu/legal-content/EN/TXT/?uri=celex%3A32008L0098

Fairphone. (2015). *Fairphone 2 production and delivery countdown!* Retrieved 16. December, 2018, from https://www.fairphone.com/en/2015/12/10/fairphone-2-production-delivery-countdown/

Fairphone. (2015). *From proud pioneer to thoughtful critic: Meet Fairphone's latest user personas.* Retrieved 10. January, 2019, from https://www.fairphone.com/de/2015/06/11/from-proud-pioneer-to-thoughtful-critic-meet-fairphones-latest-user-personas/

Fairphone. (2016). *Fairphone Fact Sheet.* Retrieved 7. January, 2019, from https://www.fairphone.com/wp-content/uploads/2016/08/Fairphone-factsheet-DE.pdf

Fairphone. (2017). *A closer look at the spare parts supply chain.* Retrieved 9. January, 2019, from https://www.fairphone.com/de/2017/08/03/a-closer-look-at-the-spare-parts-supply-chain/

Fairphone. (2017). *Fairer materials – a list of the 10 we're focusing on.* Retrieved 5. January, 2019, from https://www.fairphone.com/en/2017/02/01/fairer-materials-a-list-of-the-next-10-were-taking-on/

Fairphone. (2017). *Fairphone 2 demonstrates how modularity can drive greater sustainability.* Retrieved 9. January, 2019, from https://www.fairphone.com/wp-content/uploads/2017/02/MWCpressrelease-1.pdf

Fairphone. (2017). *Understanding the materials in mobile phones.* Retrieved 3. January, 2019, from https://www.fairphone.com/en/project/understanding-materials-mobile-phones/

Fairphone. (2018). Retrieved 7. December, 2018, from https://www.fairphone.com/en/

Fairphone. (2019). *Fairphone 2 Garantie*. Retrieved 9. January, 2019, from https://www.fairphone.com/de/legal/fairphone-2-garantie/#ihrengarantieanspruchgeltendmachen

Figge, F., Young, W., & Barkemeyer, R. (2014). Sufficiency or efficiency to achieve lower resource consumption and emissions? The role of the rebound effect. *Journal of Cleaner Production, 69*, pp. 216-224.

Geissdoerfer, M., Savaget, P., Bocken, N., & Hultink, E. (2017). The Circular Economy–A new sustainability paradigm? *Journal of cleaner production 143*, pp. 757-768.

Ghisellini, P., Cialani, C., & Ulgiati, S. (2016). A review on circular economy: the expected transition to a balanced interplay of environmental and economic systems. *Journal of Cleaner production, 114*, pp. 11-32.

Hahler, S., & Fleischmann, M. (2017). Strategic grading in the product acquisition process of a reverse supply chain. *Production and Operations Management, 26(8)*, pp. 1498-1511.

Lewandowski, M. (2016). Designing the business models for circular economy—Towards the conceptual framework. *Sustainability, 8(1)*, p. 43.

Lieder, M., & Rashid, A. (2016). Towards circular economy implementation: a comprehensive review in context of manufacturing industry. *Journal of Cleaner Production 115*, pp. 36-51.

Lunn, E. (2016). *Recycling your mobile phone? Beware the empty price 'promise'.* Retrieved 9. January, 2019, from https://www.theguardian.com/money/2016/apr/30/recycling-mobile-phone-price-promise-cut

Mathews, J., & Tan, H. (2011). Progress toward a circular economy in China: The drivers (and inhibitors) of eco-industrial initiative15(3). *Journal of industrial ecology*, pp. 435-457.

Mazuma Mobile. (2012). *Recycle mobile now: Mobile phones loaded with toxic chemicals*. Retrieved 20. January, 2019, from https://www.mazumamobile.com/blog/mobile-phone-news/recycle-mobile-now-mobile-phones-loaded-with-toxic-chemicals/

Mazuma Mobile. (2018). Retrieved 15. December, 2018, from https://www.mazumamobile.com/why/recycle

Mazuma Mobile. (2018). *Mazuma ReNew Phones: the New NEW in Mobile.* Retrieved 12. January, 2019, from https://www.mazumamobile.com/blog/general/renew-phones-new-new-mobile/

Mazuma Mobile. (n.d.). *Buy Sell Trade Phones, Tablets & Smartwatches.* Retrieved 10. January, 2019, from https://www.mazumamobile.com/

Mazuma Mobile. (n.d.). *Our promises.* Retrieved 3. January, 2019, from https://www.mazumamobile.com/promises

Myers, M. (2013). *Qualitative research in business and management.* Sage.

OECD. (2012). *Case Study on Critical Metals in Mobile Phones. Final Report. Organisation for Economic Cooperation and Development.* Retrieved 29. Novemver, 2018, from http://www.oecd.org/env/waste/Case%20Study%20on%20Critical%20Metals%20in%20Mobile%20Phones.pdf

Osterwalder, A. (2004). *The business model ontology: A proposition in a design science approach.* Dissertation 173, University of Lausanne, Switzerland.

Osterwalder, A., & Pigneur, Y. (2004). An ontology for e-business models. *Value creation from e-business models, 1,* pp. 65-97.

Osterwalder, A., & Pigneur, Y. (2010). *Business Model Generation.* New Jersey: John Wiley and Sons, Inc.

Osterwalder, A., Pigneur, Y., & Tucci, C. (2005). Clarifying business models: origins, present, and future of the concept. *Communications for the Association for Information Systems, 16,* pp. 1-25.

Pearce, D., & Turner, R. (1990). *Economics of natural resources and the environment.* JHU Press.

Prendeville, S., Sanders, C., Sherry, J., & Costa, F. (2014). *Circular economy: is it enough.* EcoDesign Centre, Wales. Retrieved 9. December, 2018, from http://www. edcw. org/en/resources/circulareconomy-it-enough

Prince Charles. (2015). *Prince Charles: To limit climate change we will need to see profound changes.* Retrieved 11. January, 2019, from https://www.theguardian.com/environment/2015/jul/03/prince-charles-climate-change-limit-profound-changes

Richardson, J. (2008). The business model: an integrative framework for strategy execution. *Strategic Change 17(5-6)*, pp. 133-144.

Schischke, K., Proske, M., Nissen, N., & Lang, K. (2016). Modular products: Smartphone design from a circular economy perspective. *Electronics Goes Green 2016*, pp. 1-8.

Schmitt, S. (2013). *Fairphone: Keines wie alle andern*. Retrieved 18. December, 2018, from https://www.zeit.de/2013/43/fairphone/komplettansicht

Schneider, A., Matinfar, S., Grua, E., Casado-Mansilla, D., & Cordewener, L. (2018). Towards a sustainable business model for smartphones: Combining product-service systems with modularity. *ICT4S*, pp. 82-99.

Seay, L. (2012). *What's wrong with Dodd-Frank 1502? Conflict minerals, civilian livelihoods, and the unintended consequences of western advocacy*. CGD Working Paper 284. Retrieved 3. January, 2019, from https://www.cgdev.org/publication/what%E2%80%99s-wrong-dodd-frank-1502-conflict-minerals-civilian-livelihoods-and-unintended

Simon, H. (1962). The Architecture of Complexity. *Proceedings of the American Philosophical Society, Vol. 106, No. 6*, pp. 467-482.

Spiegel Online. (2017). Retrieved 2. December, 2018, from http://www.spiegel.de/wissenschaft/natur/plastik-menschen-haben-mehr-als-8-milliarden-tonnen-produziert-a-1158676.html

Stahel, W. (1982). The product life factor. An Inquiry into the Nature of Sustainable Societies: The Role of the Private Sector. *Houston Area Research Center*, pp. 72-105.

Stahel, W., & Reday, G. (1976). The potential for substituting manpower for energy, report to the Commission of the European Communities.

Stähler, P. (2002). Business models as an unit of analysis for strategizing. *International workshop on business models Vol. 45, No. 7*, (pp. 2990-2995). Lausanne, Switzerland.

Su, B., Heshmati, A., Geng, Y., & Yu, X. (2013). A review of the circular economy in China: moving from rethoric to implementation. *J. Clean. Prod. 42*, pp. 215-277.

Teece, D. (2010). Business models, business strategy and innovation. *Long range planning, 43(2-3)*, pp. 172-194.

van Abel, B. (2018, September 26). "We're suffering from electronic anorexia". (M. Kasper-Claridge, Interviewer) Deutsche Welle. Retrieved 12. December, 2018, from https://www.dw.com/en/bas-van-abel-were-suffering-from-electronic-anorexia/a-45649263

van Abel, B. (2018, October 20). Fairphone-Gründer Bas van Abel: "Wir werden nie fertig sein". (B. Brodersen, Interviewer) Retrieved 13. December, 2018, from http://www.areamobile.de/news/48495-fairphone-gruender-bas-van-abel-wir-werden-nie-fertig-sein

Van den Berg, M., & Bakker, C. (2015). A product design framework for a circular economy. *Product Lifetimes And The Environment*, (pp. 365-379).

van der Velden, M. (2016). Design as Regulation. *International Conference on Culture, Technology, and Communication*, pp. 32-54.

Van Renswoude, K., Ten Wolde, A., & Joustra, D. (2015). *Circular Business Models - Part 1: An introduction to IMSA's circular business model scan*. Retrieved 17. December, 2018, from IMSA: Amsterdam, The Netherlands: https://groenomstilling.erhvervsstyrelsen.dk/sites/default/files/media/imsa_circular_business_models_-_april_2015_-_part_1.pdf

von Lindern, J. (2014). *Fair ist schwer*. Retrieved 11. December, 2018, from https://www.handelsblatt.com/technik/gadgets/leit-artikel-fairphone-fair-ist-schwer/9362604.html

von Lindern, J. (2016). *Fairphone: Bau mich um*. Retrieved 14. December, 2018, from https://www.zeit.de/2016/19/fairphone-handys-umwelt-technologie/komplettansicht

Wernink, T., & Strahl, C. (2015). Fairphone: sustainability from the inside-out and outside-in. *Sustainable Value Chain Management*, pp. 123-139.

Abbreviations

BB	Building Blocks
BM	Business Model
CE	Circular Economy
CR	Customer Relationship
CS	Customer Segment
C$	Cost Structure
EMF	Ellen MacArthur Foundation
KA	Key Activities
KP	Key Partnerships
KR	Key Resources
R$	Revenue Stream
VP	Value Proposition